Singing Puccini
at the kitchen sink

Bert Flitcroft

D1637865

Fineleaf

PUBLISHED BY FINELEAF, ROSS-ON-WYE
www.fineleaf.co.uk

First published 2011
Copyright © 2011 by Bert Flitcroft
ISBN   978-1-907741-03-6

Design: Philip Gray
Typeface: Bembo
Print: SS Media Ltd

Published by Fineleaf Editions, 2011
Moss Cottage, Pontshill, Ross-on-Wye HR9 5TB
www.fineleaf.co.uk   books@fineleaf.co.uk

British Library Cataloguing in Publication Data
A catalogue record for this book is available from the British Library.

Acknowledgements

To Bob Mee and Jonathan Davidson, for their advice and
encouragement,
to my fellow poets in friendship, for their invaluable
comments,
and to my wife Hilary, who can spot a bad line before
I've even written it.

A number of these poems have been published in
magazines and anthologies or have been short-listed in
poetry competitions. *Revisiting, Still Scene, Think of it (as
Dry Dock)* and *Bamburgh* were published in Envoi; *Internal*
was published in iota; *Kite* was published in Raw Edge;
First Time was published in Obsessed with Pipe Work.
The poems *Alrewas* and *Landlubbers cruising the Great
Glen* appeared in the anthology Nothing Left to Burn
from Ragged Raven Press. *On the Edge* was selected and
appeared in the Blinking Eye competition anthology
Night Balancing. *Night Life, Spa Man* and *Standing
in front of Turner's Norham Castle* have all been short-
listed for the Bridport Prize. *Sonnet to a Bacon Sandwich*
was a Midland's prize-winner in the Faber-Ottaker
competition and *Eye to Eye* was commended in the
Stafford Poetry Competition. Other poems have been
short-listed in Housman Society competitions.

Contents

Equilibrium

I am beginning to see precisely
how opposite poles attract
while like particles   repel each other.

And how the laws of motion:
that action   and reaction
are always equal   and opposite,
must be universal.

It's how we heave metal   into the air
and keep it flying there.
It's why the moon and romance
keep circling the earth,
why we hug the sun
instead of careering off towards Andromeda,
or Vega,   or god-knows-where.

So I guess that you and me, our life, is this.
A balancing,   governed by the same laws
that pull   and push the tides,

as if we were some sort of global weather map,
my high pressure balancing   your low,
my warm fronts following   your cool.

It would be so easy,   if we were too casual,
to see us flying off   flailing our arms,
unbalanced   and uprooted by winds.

Landlubbers cruising The Great Glen

Out on the loch that feels deeper
                                   and darker
                                              than thought

we knuckle our way, hands
                          clamped to the wheel,
                                                down the funnel of wind

that whips away the not-lashed-down.

We lift and fall, and bash a path
                                   through the body of
                                                       cresting waves.

We pitch and roll our tongues
                              around the meaning of yaw
                                                        and hitch,
learn the language of ropes.

We sleep in the wedge
                      of the hollow bow
                                        like marionettes,

my head at twenty five past,
                             yours at twenty five to.

We slip through a discourse of days.

We drift in and out of dawns,
                              waves slapping the edge
                                                     of dreams.
Water,

water rippling the wind,
                         caressing
                                   the egg-shell hull,
                                                      soothing,
erasing
until our ears, our eyes no longer know
the language of ground,
the sound of hills,
the meaning of hearth.

Bridge across the Estuary

The black rocks anchored once
their lobster pots, their fishing nets,
just below the picnic site we found by chance,
down an unmarked village lane that butts
the estuary wall,
where wind-blown machair clings to the silt,
salt gulls wheeling over tidal flats.

The tables are scrubbed, grass is kept short.
Information is displayed in perspex
about the history of ferry crossings here,
how horse-drawn carriages tumbled
into sweeping currents,
graphic tales of graphic drownings.

The railway had built the wooden piers,
used local fishermen who knew
the channels, the eddies, the shifting banks,
to embark ladies in their fur stoles.
Until the engineers burrowed their tunnel
and left the groynes to slide into the mud,
left men to eke out livelihoods
with flatfish and flounder.

Until the road bridge came, that is,
looping its steel web across the skyline
to straddle the tidal surge,
and threw the family of fishermen
into their silent isolation.

Breathtaking.
The way it strides across the estuary.
The sense of space.
The black rocks.

On the Edge

The closest I'll come
to walking on the moon – that feeling,
came like a gift on top of Applecross,
with a few small steps from the road
onto sterile crags of rock that jut
and plummet and undulate away.

The urge was strong to walk, and walk,
to stride to where the wide sky loomed,
stretched like a tight skin
over this spinning lump of rock
held gently by the sun,
towards the edge you never reach.

I saw the first small step, you know;
the giant leap,
space suits bouncing like bubbles,
stars and stripes against a black sky,
stiff in the moon's breeze.

Armstrong must look up on clear nights,
still see the virgin dust scuffed,
the small craters of his footprints
just as he left them,
unchanged, and waiting.

He must have felt like this,
this wanting to walk alone and free,
until his air just.... petered out.
Knowing the rock's indifference.
Content. Just to be part of it.

Inheritance

Not what they had.
Piece-work, lip-reading over looms in the cotton mill;
no bank account, no will to be read at the funeral.
No trace of an exotic family tree,
no silver fob and albert with a history to tell.

But what they knew.
Some arcane, grown-up formula for living
without complaint, and understanding
that love is about giving more than you take.
That children shouldn't answer back,
or cheat, or steal sweets from the corner shop.
How to make time for the widow up the street;
the value of sixpence for a loaf of bread.

And, naturally, the genes.
Ginger whiskers, I'm told, from an uncle
I was named after, killed in the war.
My father's deep-set laughter lines,
his eyebrows, the way he walked,
the way he sang Puccini at the kitchen sink.
And I can hear, just now, how the past comes true.
More and more, his intonation, a turn of phrase
 I catch myself using on the stairs.

All part of the formula I'm still working out,
although I know I will leave
more than they had:
bricks and mortar, some books,
some seventies furniture.
With luck, a memory or two of a father having fun,
cart-wheeling or on a swing dressed as Superman.

Kite

My eldest, who fell into the nettle patch
and ran home crying,
who split her scalp like a peach
on the piano's edge,
sat friendless on the playground,

is here now sitting at her screen.
I watch her tap-dancing the keys,
finding the model just right for me.

And when it arrives it is perfect:
three metre span, power enough
to drag a man along the sands,
to grapple with the moorland winds.

She unfolds it without fuss,
unfurls pockets, unwinds strings
orange and green across the field.
I follow, uncoiling, copying
her deft magician's hands.

She shows me how to grip,
how to climb and swoop,
how to brake, bring down
the kite with gentleness.

When I take the reins – I feel
the sudden power snatch, and
feel her safe hands hold me down.
I let her strong arms guide me,
show me how to use the wind
to control the life above us,
how to handle all the turbulence.

Handing over
on a stroll up to the butchers

What does a father say,
when he has his doubts?
The man comes with baggage
and talks about his motorcycle trip
next year around Algeria.
This doesn't square with the thought
of settling down,
shared bank accounts, a nursery.

I know they love each other, have fun.
I give him my approval
with a formal handshake
as if to seal the deal
on a second-hand Jag.
And when it is done I realise
I am pleased, and glad
that he asked – the implied respect.

Afterwards it dawns on me –
I didn't ask. We just announced it
over the steak and chips,
without the man-to-man, the handshake.
Forty years ago,
and it never occurred to me.
Did he resent it?
He might have said no.

Settling

I remember it. Fourteen, on Mont Ventoux,
when the earth first unfurled before you,
revealed itself as all yours.
Since then I've watched the all-weather years
you've spent on the moors, cutting and coring
the black peat, revealing
the minute secrets of their seed-heads,
how the early hunter gatherers lived.
Adding to the sum of knowledge.
Revelling in it.

So how did you become so in-grown,
busy careering down the domestic years?
I watch you pause by the stove,
lift the hem of an apron in that classic pose
to wipe your hands, and browse
the pages of your countryside calendar,
as if you've settled for a windowsill
of potted thyme and dill and marjoram.

I see how you prepare your artichokes,
cutting each one deliberately, slowly
through to the heart, to the taste of it.
In the unkempt cellar beneath your feet
tyres on a mountain bike are kept inflated.
Climbing ropes hang in rows like bell-pulls.

Calling from New Zealand

"I've arrived. I'm calling from New Zealand."
And there's a pause.
Outside I can hear a blackbird's song,
next door's lawn mower.
And down the line your voice,
the shapes and intonation of your words,
are clear as spring water.
I'm surprised by the absence of crackle,
the sound of operators' voices,
the unanswerable noises of distance.

You're just having a coffee, you say,
and my cup on the table is suddenly yours,
and through the lounge window I can see
figures surfing on the beach below.

Calling from New Zealand.
Your voice is just the same, unchanged
by thousands of miles I can't start to imagine.
And mine is lifted knowing you have made it.

I am trying not to sound like a parent,
an anxious parent
with a hundred questions,
wanting, yet not wanting,
to ask how you really are – the personal stuff.

Behind your words
there's the hollow sound of an empty flat.
I can see you standing there;
the absence of chairs, bare floorboards,
the phone in your hand.

A present to Bert

straight from Lijiang, a thumb-length
printing block of boxwood, dense as ivory,
carved by hand with images
of tendrils and a leaping tiger.
And on the bottom square, four symbols,
precise and perfect, etched
by an ancient artisan in tangerine and sandals,
sitting cross-legged on a bamboo porch.

I'm told they're Mandarin.
With hands and sounds they asked him
to carve my name – enunciated it
with lips and tongue placed plosively,
until his eyes lit up.

I hold its smooth weight like a nugget
in the palm of my hand, turn it over,
run my fingers across the grooves
feeling my name, 'Bert' in Mandarin.

They tested it – on a farmer in a paddy field,
on a couple on the overnight Beijing Express,
on a waiter serving charcoaled crickets on sticks.
'Ah! Bert' they all pronounced. In Mandarin,
the sound of my name. Amazing.

When writing I try to hone my images as skilfully.
I'm tempted to stamp my name,
to 'block it' or 'chop it', as they say,
in red at the foot of the page.
Bert – in Mandarin.

I don't. Much too pretentious.
But I could. I'd like to, really.

Notes on a napkin

I argued (over dinner) that words
and poetry were all we needed,
that they were nuclear; like neutron
particles we could explode or fuse
to divine the trajectories of our lives,
to show how far we've come,
how far we have to go.

On a linen napkin you wrote, and said,
that 'we can measure the distance
a body has travelled in its lifetime;
can prove that this is equal
to its initial velocity
times
the time of its journey
plus half
of its acceleration
times
time squared.'

And these were merely noises in the ear.
Approximations. Sounds
that might as well be Greek or Ukrainian.

On the other side you jotted down,
$s = u\,t + \frac{1}{2}\,f\,t^2$.
Precise. Transforming.
The poetry of Newton, Euclid, Faraday.

Formula

Imagine that a Royal Astronomer one night
(for argument's sake let's call him Isaac)
trips, and falls from a turret
clutching his telescope.
Would he, cool as you like, accept
his number was up, knowing
that he would plummet
at a speed which equals
his initial velocity
plus his acceleration
multiplied by
the time he spends in the air?

Or would he, in this time of tumbling stars
think of his good wife at home
and pray for a miracle, someone below
with a blanket or a wagon of straw
to break his fall,
and deduce a scientific formula for love
to prove the relative force of it
before it is   extinguished?

Nightlife

After the News, before your Horlicks
and my two fingers of Laphroaig,
I switch off all the lights, pull back
the curtains that velvet our picture window.

Out in the dark the wild cherry tree
like Cerberus with its three twisted trunks
is guarding the end of the garden,
its branches tapping warnings on the fence.

Out in the dark the lawn is stretching
its edges like lips around a yawn,
shaping the bites of Peone and Potentilla,
surrounding the pond where mottled carp
are finning their shapes through the ink.

Out in the dark the feeding bat
is cross-stitching the hidden stars.
The hedgehog is trekking its path,
sniffing beneath the laurel and the holly.
Whatever night brings, scuffing the patio wall
it stalks at the edge of things.

Sometimes, you come and rest your fingers
on the glass, testing the membrane
that partitions the dark, leaving
the smudge of your whorls for the daylight.

Sonnet to a Bacon Sandwich

You, with a nappy gripped in one hand,
flung the plate over my head.
I remember how the white bread
took its own trajectory like a startled bird.
You yelled something about pulling and weight.
Me? I was at the table waiting to be fed.
Hadn't I been working all day?
And wasn't that the wife's job anyway?
These days, at each anniversary we still
chew over that bacon sandwich,
our only serious row, and how
we both had to learn to cut off the rind,
to butter each other's bread from time to time.
To listen for the spitting under the grill.

Bamburgh

Though we have no photos
I remember the jelly-like sands,

a tassel beneath dark castle walls,
how the tide surged between our toes,

the shrieks as tentacles of seaweed
ropes chased our girls in shorts.

How gulls bobbed teasingly on the swell
like fairground targets in a heaving line,

how the surf drowned out all sounds
that washed between us and the dunes,

how the waves would gently slide,
their endless renewal making

more peaceful my peace,
my stillness more still.

Odd, how the mind selects
which images remain, then

pops one up now and again,
like a poem on a page.

You are sketching a shell,
scratching on cartridge, practising
your passion, your skill.

An education

The only thing I remember from my art lessons
is the teacher hurling a board duster at a boy
who was masturbating on the back row.
I was trying to draw a cow, and didn't know

how to attach the legs to the body.
I still don't, so I've decided to learn to draw.
My wife is helping me. She says
"It's just about seeing, using your eyes."

So I'll be fretting about the holiday money,
or a drainpipe, or the pain in my left bunion,
and she'll say, "Look at the yellowhammers,
over there, by the patch of Lady's Bedstraw."

Or "Look at the butterflies, the purple buddleia."
Funny, how you can live together and be so different.
It's as if, at times, we inhabit separate universes.
Like the boy on the back row and the art teacher.

Facing up

So here I am. Submitting,
my back pinned stiff as a rod
to the chair, hands resting
soft as wilting petals.

A woman in pink is pointing
her pencil like a pistol
at my head,
tracing me into the air.
She is sketching the lines
that gravity has etched
into my moon-smooth face.

An engineer who likes to draw machines
scales me down with his brush,
measures me by closing one eye,
holding up his thumb
like Caesar on a good day.

No more excuses now –
it's the strip light in the bathroom,
or it's just the angle of the sun.

I am out there, beyond
the boundaries of my illusions,
steeling myself.

Country girl

....and from the first, she was bowled over
by the poetry of city life, converted

by the crazy diction of its pavements,
the babble of phrases spilling out of bars,
the monologues of menus.

She breathed in pastoral anthologies
of local parks; the quatrains of squares
with their sibilance of fountains.

She learned to read the ink of urban canals
writing their elegies to engineers,
and something in her shifted....

First Contact

When contact comes, it is not white noise
or the pulse of a radio wave.
It is not from a star-wars ship of titanium.
But it comes from the deep,
an unseen force that pulls an invisible line
from a parallel, liquid universe.
And it comes to the lure of a damsel nymph
or a deer-hair wing.

I have known the moment, the tearing meniscus,
the shock
of first contact that shoots
up a carbon rod to a forged steel reel
and into your hand, your muscle and bone,
and into your mind.

And then the creature, leaping through
from the other side, bursting into our air.
There is a tug of wills, the instinct to live.
It runs and pulls,
and then there's the landing,
each scale-skin touching I never forget.

Wind farm

They have settled in a few small colonies,
put down roots deep in the bedrock
where the wind can dance around them.
They push and pull the thinning air,
are pushed and pulled in symbiotic motion,
like children endlessly cart-wheeling
or freewheeling down the long hill home
through the fabric of space time.

There is something of the stars about them;
some deep-space, silicon-based life form,
their sleek grey skin impervious
to cold and rain and virus.
Their Godless, nacelle heads are peering
over hills, or brazening it out on peaty moors
like alien outposts, not quite of this world.

For all we know something dark inside
them may be fretting, something stark
and tongueless, poised.

At Goodrich Castle

Even now the air still shapes their rooms.
You can almost taste the swan, the nettles, turnips.
You can hear the hoof beats of a warhorse,
the crows at dawn cawing over the river,
love songs from the strings of a plaintive lyre.
You can imagine their lives, the difference.

After my burning and scattering
you must leave something of me embedded
in such stone. My descendants might visit.
They could imagine my box-like house,
my rows of books, the dog in his basket.
Me at an upstairs window looking down
on my lawn, the rockery, the garden wall.

Alrewas

There's no way back to ancestors.
We cannot eat their crude bread, their meat,
nor breathe their air. And yet we can return,
beyond the archives to the ancient place
for we are of their time as well as ours.

I have stood by the river's edge and watched
the hunters leave, take their arrowheads
and skins, and follow the tracks of wolves.
I have seen the gatherers move in, fan out,
fell trees, and set their boundaries.

A few apologetic scraps of thatch remain,
a few old beams and timber frames leaning
like ironic exclamation marks;
but it was they who gave this place a name,
the settlement by water and by wood.

And you cannot obliterate a settlement.
Isolation is not possible where rivers are.
I have cowered in the reeds and seen the Trent
give birth to long-ships in the morning mist,
trembled as their hordes laid waste the mickleholme.

I have seen how the weight of waters balanced
as we joined the river at the hip to a slit of sky
where now the narrow boats come gliding in,
all cruising the possibilities like dogs let out
at first light onto the village green.

We have embraced old names, and what they were.
Walkfield, and Oakfield, and Essington;
a well, a mill, and a furlong to measure out.
I have dreamed of the fox still padding the lane
when the village beds down for the darkness.

Though we are a fragment fallen from a moment
it does not seem so. There are memories of
memories; and brooches and burial mounds.
There are names, always names, that outlast bones.
This place is still their place. And it is ours.

Be there

Stroll down Daisy Lane and over the by-pass.
Down Common Lane there's a single Chestnut
left in the centre of a thistle-spiked field.
The copse of its mates has been uprooted.

It's a full-grown muscular tree, held firm
by rock-deep roots. Part of the land,
it bends with the heave and pull of gales,
its speckled crown a fingerprint all its own.

It's doing what trees do – sunbathing,
sheltering finches, sugaring its leaves,
shedding them; defying lightning, hoar-frosts
and darkness until the spring arrives.

Be there, when the heavy-duty diggers come.
Old trees stand witness. Their creed is soil
and water; they know the screech-owl's claw,
the stoat, the scrabbling sounds of midnight.

Statue at the National Memorial Arboretum

Figures cast in bronze or carved in oak
leave me indifferent.
I see no sadness in stone,
no beauty in Graces, or gargoyles,
or polar bears on plinths quarried
from cold-sores on the earth's skin.
No grief in the chiselling of names.

For me, it is the sundown fading of a bugle,
the quiet breath of words.

Yet, look at this white figure by the river,
trench coat hanging from stiff shoulders,
hands manacled behind a post,
strips of cloth across his eyes.
A regimental fusilier perhaps;
a private, enduring
knots in the stomach, the soiling;
a baker's boy with a bicycle;
a trembling clerk shot for his refusal.
He is all of these.

And this is how it was.
The boot emerging somehow
from the stone into today
moves me back
down the line
into a birdless dawn
poised
for the barking of the order,
the crack of bullets to pierce the envelope.

At Chepstow Castle

They must have found it fat and teeming,
those pioneers – the forests, the fertile land
they burned and cleared as they settled in.
They built this castle and keep to last.

I am spellbound by their competence
with hewn and huge and hoisted blocks of stone,
how they perched them on the edge of this cliff;
by the damp and darkness of its dungeon,
with the lingering sense of danger.

Such brief and urgent lives spent wonderfully:
scratching scurvy skin,
bitten by lice in straw-filled beds,
plagued by brittle bones that cracked with cold,
or bent like their spiralling stairs.

I am drawn to this,
to run my fingertips along this pitted wall,
to touch the fabric of lives rubbed raw
and fearful, yet somehow glorious.

Standing in front of Turner's 'Norham Castle'

How his eyes that morning must have felt immersed,
must have deep-breathed in
this mist, this buttercup sun
sponging into a champagne sky.
How his eager hands must have been impatient
to unpeel, to capture, this glorious fruit
the gods had given him.

It seems the earth he knew was dissolving.
Not a single line of thatch to etch the emptiness.
Not a single daub of a boat to give relief.
Bankside trees are bleached invisible
and Norham Castle is adrift in haze.
Just one solitary butterscotch cow,
with its head down,
hooves planted in the river's pond,
roots us with the map of her flanks.

I've seen this light,
felt the push of its glare against my eyes.
In Beadnell Bay it was, with the tide well out.
I stood at the water's edge, squinting
as a seal might if lifted from her element
and asked to swim in the bright air,
the skin of the sea suddenly beneath her,
the sea bed's certainty removed.

It made me wary that the tide might wash
unseen and creep behind me, be waiting
as I turned my eyes to where the dunes,
the clumps of marram grass, should be.

Tug Master 1838 *(after J.M.W. Turner)*

So, the Temeraire has given up the ghost.
No creaking timbers now at night
groaning with their salty task.
No wooden masts to splinter under siege.
No ship's carpenters with nails
between their lips like splintered teeth,
their desperate hands planing and sawing
and clouting to keep out the heaving seas.

The world is iron now.
Look at the beauty of this iron hull,
how it parts the swell until the sea
lies flat and weak beneath its will.
My legs tremble with the hiss of steam,
the push of pistons driven by white-hot fire,
the way smoke belches from its throat,
blotting out the sun.

The man who nips and tucks

The brazen ones arrive at noon,
their shades and headscarves
like beacons in the gloom.
Some knock on my heavy door at dusk.
Always, they move from foot to foot
on my white rug, pause to admire
my glass table, my Persian carpet,
hesitate before the Queen Anne chairs.

I am an artist. My easel is a sterile table.
My canvas is made of living cells.
My pen can sweep a perfect line
beneath a chin, trace a perfect curve
around a breast, over an eyebrow.

My scalpel is more lethal
than a sculptor's chisel,
more daring than a painter's brush.
Afterwards I watch them, my models,
open their eyes in fear and hope,
run their fingers over surprising scars.

Sometimes I am a writer. I write short stories,
create new characters and new beginnings.
My plots are the pock-marked surfaces of life.
I scatter lies, illusions, like leaves around them.
Who am I to judge?

Soaking in my bath, toeing my gold taps,
I dream of beads of blood
glistening with the first incision;
twisted metal, smooth rejuvenated skin.
I see symmetry. The face of Venus,
perfect buttocks, the pink ears of pigs.

Buxton Man

I read this poem once, and it's come true.
There's an ape in the house next door.
He's as muscle bound as celery,
and he roars.
His voice is iron – inviolable
and his music throbs, competing
with his fucking this and fucking that,
piercing the thick Victorian walls,
the sound proofing,
roaring and head-banging around my room.

I witness late and early his assertion.
He roars at the mice.
He roars at Bugs Bunny.
He roars at his girlfriend for staying out late,
as if deep down
he needs to be the loudest,
a sort of simian town crier striving
for what he was or what he could be,
if only the world would stand aside.
But it doesn't. And it won't.

At night I imagine him lost in the Gobi,
roaring across the dunes
while a string of big-eyed camels
raise their heads and stare in amazement.

Finished

When it finally arrived,
my farewell speech,
imagining the gift of a carriage clock
or bone china tea cups I would never use,
(or a fishing rod, as it turned out),
how hard it was
to admit to such diminished interest,
to confess to such diminished energy,
the run-down batteries.

How hard it had been to hide,
to be a faded photocopy of myself,
to feel the push of the young, their certainty.
To have no stomach for those endless meetings,
studying the scuff marks on the wall
as words and moisture drops on window frames
leach out into the winter afternoons.

All those words, criss-crossing like atoms
in some random act of fusion.
All those awkward silences,
those pauses,
when you've spoken and hit the mark.
Or missed.
All those years of aiming.

I know she's your mother, but...

Too Industrial

She sees your glamour next to my flat cap,
hears my flat vowels next to your plum,
and even now they prompt those pursed lips,
those sly, raised eyebrows in company.
Too northern, you see; not the yachting type
she'd always wanted you to marry.

'Does he take sugar?'
Looking at you, stirring ,
her teaspoon clinking the last drops
into the whirlpool,
as if her memory had let her down.
Bristling, I bite my tongue, say nothing.
I can imagine her calling her father 'Sir',
can see her sitting on her hands in silence
at the breakfast table, at afternoon tea.
Left to herself in the nursery.

Maybe it's in the genes, like the kink
in the left ear passed down to her granddaughters.
You've told me how she pinched you
once, in temper, hard.
You call her 'Mother'
and I see her arms hang like plumb lines
when you peck her cheek to leave.

Revisiting

Months since we last came, we re-map the place;
each room, each photo the same. Out back
thick branches arch over the old lawn.
Moss and dandelion fill out thin grass.

Head down, she slurps her tea,
thin lips reaching for the rattling cup.
Daffodils droop from a white vase,
wax stems softening in the warm air.

Her Ken is bending over the heavy chair,
hands gripping the wooden slats,
swinging the weight from leg to leg,
walking it, by inches, into line.

Without thought, I sit bolt upright,
straighten my spine.

Internal

She has skipped through buttercup
fields on the edge of town,
waltzed below ground while bombs
shuddered above,
loved, had you,
has buried him.
All this, and years in Accounts,
all counting for nothing,
reduced to an invisible friend.

"No but we were always out,
dancing.
He was a quiet man,
hated hot weather.
During the war he worried
about being sent to Borneo,
said he'd die of the heat.
No but he did like to dress up
in his dinner suit."

Her head is crammed
with reported speech
that tumbles out.
It isn't the gift of a jam sponge
from a widowed friend she recalls,
but the chat
about her cataracts, the rain.
She breathes
in who says what and when.
She breathes
out how she replied,
recites whole conversations.

"No but my friend Jean up the road,
she's sixty eight bless her,
invited us in and she said,
do you know what it says in the Old Testament?
and I said no, what does it say, I said.
It says wine gladdens the heart, she said,
and in Paul's letter to Timothy, she said,
it says, take a little wine for thy stomach's sake.
So I said, does it really? I said,
and she said, Yes. Let's have a drink! she said.
So we did, and when I got back home
I looked it up and underlined it."

Often, at tea some internal dialogue
bursts through the crust
of her subconscious, overflows
like a riposte into our day,
dumbfounding us with how a fox
climbs to that garage roof to sunbathe,
how that chap in number forty six,
poor man, must live on frozen chips.

❖

Vase

Classic curves, deep ruby red,
it took up residence long ago
beside her photographs,
belongs there now, its cool emptiness
dramatic
on the oak-stained gate-leg table
by the veil of lace net curtains.

It should be giving birth, this vase;
was breath-blown and shaped
to cradle the faces of red roses
that would warm the room, fill it
with their quiet contemplation.

It should be pushing up the stems of tulips,
their bell-cups opening, high-petalling
to see the widow from the flat below
tending her polyanthus, her geraniums,
her late-flowering dahlias that bow
and speak to her with their soft spikes.

Forty years on

Still the son-in-law who won't quite do.
"Would he like…? Is he coming in?"

Still unopened, the whisky and gin
in the chilled front room.

Still, the too-easy cheque at Christmas
wrapped in a small brown envelope.

Still, at lunch the only empty glass,
wine in the bottle left unpoured.

Still bare walls; no pictures, no art,
just standing family photos I'm not in.

Still, the hollowing cheek unkissed,
blue-marbled hands I've never touched.

Flying Club

We were 'spreading our wings'
for the weekend, the usual banter
lifting us with laughter, with thoughts
of hotel beds and baths and evening gowns,
knowing a gin and tonic or two
would undo the tight buttons of our lives.

We joked about the sign, the Flying Club
holding their dinner in the Palace Suite,
imagined waltzing with officers' wives,
the deep-pile corridors as long as runways
and Spitfires climbing in formation,
propellers and 'chocks away' before
that lean-back moment of lift off.

At dawn, when the drone of Lancasters
returning safe from their bombing run
might sound against the rising sun,
we saw their squadron of flat caps,
their breakfast plates piled high
with beans, black pudding and fried bread.
Pennine vowels drifted with the smell of bacon,
and snatches of excited conversation...
diet...seed...racing....champion...
and that open-basket moment of release.

You could see the tight skin of their lives
relaxing as they pictured pigeons winging
into the ice-blue air unchecked,
the miracle of how they circle and circle,
home in, then head for the familiar coop,
the joy of touching down, coming home.

Glad

All night she must have sat, stiffening
in the dim-yellow dining room light,
the dome of her back, her bent spine,
and the thin skittles of her brittle bones
slumped in the chair.

It isn't only the death that upsets;
it's the dying – the surge and squall of it,
the roll of thunder.
I'm glad I knew her in her upright, sexy days,
knew the true depth and cadence of her voice.
Better to think of her just nodding off
among her figurines and teacups,
motes drifting like tiny angels
in the early morning sun.

Here, in this bone-cold church,
her name has already dislodged itself,
the lines of her stone-cold forehead
have written their testament
to that terrible, final absence.

A life of work and war and men, shrunk
to this wooden box. It seems so small.

Much too young

Her best friend, dressed in poppy red, summed up
her quirks, her talents, and her zest for life.
An uncle recalled her pony, her pigtails – all that.
Her distressed mother stumbled over the eulogy
and cried at the injustice – at the cold fact of it.

"When I go, no-one should pray," she'd said.
So there were no prayers, no hymns, in the new chapel
with its pews and panelling of pale young wood.
Just these few memories and anecdotes striving
to swell and satisfy the afternoon air.

I thought of my father's coffin: its heaviness,
the horizons of its sides as I peered in,
the revelation of my own outburst of prayer.
The surprise of his mouth so relaxed, his hair
parted and combed as if nothing had changed.

Conversation at The Feathers

I'm sipping my daily Earl Grey, without milk,
in the lounge of an old coaching-house hotel,
when the conversation turns to doctors:
how they should be made to write poetry,
how they no longer need, as part of their training,
to work with dead bodies.
This doesn't sound very reassuring.

There are crumbs from cakes and scones
scattered on the cushion of a red settee,
clinging to the edges of a hollow
left by the buttocks of a woman
a few minutes earlier.
I try to rewind, but can't. In a pause,
I ask, "Why are we talking about this?"

Almost

Across the empty coffee cups and ferns,
caught unawares I was ensnared, my eyes
held by the shock of coal-black hair
that framed her milk-white face,
the perfect curve of her pale brow,
two pencil-line eaves, a fine nose.
Everything precise, composed.
Her hands soft on her wheelchair's
black and bloated tyres.

And a wedding ring of white gold.
I could have envied him, almost,
lifting her each morning from her bed,
his arms cushioning the lumps of her spine,
his arms full with the weight of his love.

Breaking

I am silent, and soothed by this glide
between trees, by the rhythm
of rails and occasional diamonds of points,
the steady pulse of sun between poles.

Frost is clinging to the rutted fields,
fine mist whispering over murky ponds.
Leaves are wrestling with the push of air
as we bullet our separate ways through the day.

A twisted spire slides across the empty sky,
then slips away.......... and I am still.
In the black of tunnels figures stare
like ghosts the sun has failed to drown,

and there in the haunting glass with my own
your face keeps following....keeps following....
Each kiss of the brakes, each gentle slowing,
is their warm closing, our final embrace.

Something in the air

That dawn, suspended over the silver rails
of steel, those thin, charged wires buzzed
as if they were excited by some secret in the air.

You stood alone, a figure in a still scene
drawn to wait at the platform's edge,
your shoes like commas on the painted line.

Your eyes were smiling, gazing across the tracks
to where she lingered, waiting to wave.
Drizzle settled softly on your sleeve, unnoticed.

Above you, on the silhouetted gantry,
one red light winked, and paused,
and the green light blazed.

Just another moment of epiphany
on my way to work

It was the trees. Just the trees, that's all.
Nothing to do with rituals or God,
or tribulation, or my soul.
At dawn the light pushed in like a high tide
drowning the night sky, and over the land
it deepened into a sea of white.
Across the fields poplars pointed a flotilla of masts.
Alders waved their regatta of flags
as if in celebration of first Autumn mist.
The birth of a season.   A dawning.
Earth was still warm, Atmosphere cooling.
Hemispheres were tilting.

Today

It is February 1st and biting cold outside.
They are out there squabbling again,
the sparrows, flitting in and out of the holly
to the peanuts and seeds.
There must be twenty of them.
Two are bullying the rest
and fighting with each other
for the nuts and crusts of bread.

This morning's newspaper is propped up
against the coffee pot and muesli.
Its front-page headline shocks us
with the 'tragic' death of a teenage boy,
shot in his own bed by a rival gang.

Page two outlines a civil court case,
a feud between a brother and sister.
She inherited the family firm by forging
their father's will, he claims.
He seems to be an innocent.
She has, it reads, 'substantial natural cunning.'

They are still manoeuvring out there,
with insistent beaks and fluttering wings,
at the edge of the lawn where history is seconds old,
darting from the holly leaves
for those few remaining scraps of bacon fat.

Eye to eye

I was rounding a bend on the Tamworth road,
down into third, tread gripping the curve,
when a white smudge shaped itself into a swan.
She must have glided in, touched down
on the verge, and sidled into the stream
to find the tarmac surface unforgiving,
her webbed feet moulding to the pitted stone.

I have always swerved, or lifted my foot
to distance the tyres' crunching of bones.
I have never smacked the haunch of a cow
on its morning walk to the milking shed,
nor stroked the scales of a grass snake.
Through fear I suppose, or lack of curiosity.

Yet there she was, investigating the white line.
Her rump ticked off each measured stride
towards the body of this hesitating car,
and my small face safe behind its smeared screen.
Until her soft down breasted a staring headlight,
pushed against the glass-smooth eye, testing.

It is with me still, that moment, pure as air.
She must have felt the idling, trembling engine
as she eased herself erect, her long neck reaching
as she flaunted the span of her wings,
her natural place in the scheme of things,
the beautiful, animal power of her undercarriage.

Still-life – Bay of Naples

Picture it, a pastel-painted, grand hotel.
Balconies laced with towels draped in the sun.

Clusters of sun-burnt bodies around
blue pools, by a landscaped garden.

Look at the palms, how their thick trunks
sprout parasols of feathered leaves.

Look at the fruit trees, in measured lines,
how they scatter their freckled patterns.

See the way their polished leaves curl
to shelter their swollen grapefruit

and their modest limes, from wilting heat.
Look, how the lemons seem to hang,

lustrous, like perfect tears
on the hot cheek of the afternoon.

The Remarkables

They are pleased to be without near-neighbours,
these isolated, elongated islands,
and almost too excited by their own geology.

It is the paradox of scale that dominates:
too many lakes and mountains to take in,
all somewhere north of this or south of that.

Early settlers foraged for the Hurunui's harvest,
fought for every clearing. Later they would have
red roses in full bloom alongside daffodils.

And lawns and tearooms at the Rotorua croquet club.
Cold southerlies, blowing in that sense of 'otherness'
as you lie in bed listening, your English toes pointing
to the Pacific just across the road.

Books and their covers

I am reading by the canal,
a land of bull-rushes and boats
and lawns edging the water.
Then, over one shoulder – he's there
striding past like half an angry argument,
walking it off, in a world of his own.
A shaven-headed, tattooed
bull-necked Minotaur of a man
racing away down the tow path.

He is pushing a pink buggy
with tiny wheels and plastic struts
you'd think his ham fists would crush,
and there were twins in it.
His two little princesses,
two round cream faces, bonneted
and bumping along shoulder to shoulder.

Think of it

An engineer, he worked on boats.
Two years ago his busy hands
were steeped in oil and bilge
tending the diesel beat of engines;
spending damp days healing wounds
by fusing metal skin with blue flames;
fixing broken screws or rusted bolts;
scouring pitted, ageing hulls;
nursing barges in their dry beds.

I watch him hobble to the local shop.
Iron-willed, he walks with sticks
as knotted as the knuckles he cannot bend,
knees as stiff as rudders bound with rope.
He's still afloat, held steady by ceramic hips,
fitted out with rods of steel
secured by screws to brittle bone,
often stranded in dry-dock.
A man-of-war, weathering the storm;
counting down, adding up, the anaesthetics.

All Souls

It was a shock, going back,
to see the terraced rows, the yards
and the air-raid shelters swept away,
the soot-blackened church still there
where my sister married a carpenter,
the boy of her dreams.

To see its stained windows so besieged,
the barbed-wire mindset,
the message board with times for Evensong
anachronistic amid the salwar kameez,
the Sky dishes,
the littered debris of half a century.

I imagined the vicar on twitter
awaiting a sign from on high,
a tweet instructing him to open the doors,
to let back in the fishermen,
the labourers, the thieves,
the sewers of seeds.
To try it for forty days.

Mr Duckworth

Mr. Duckworth was just so fat.
In slippers he would sit on his step
to watch the girls play tig, the boys
kick a tennis ball against his red-brick wall.
But something died with him:
the Sunday hand-bell of an ice-cream van,
the spark from cobbles and clogs,
the doorstep streaks of donkey stone.

Our fluted gas-lamp wicket
turned into a concrete sodium glare.
Houses cower now beneath its yellow eye.
They have gritted over the hopscotch,
spirited away the hoops and humming tops.
All ginnels and doors stay shut down the street.
Two solid ranks of cars stand guard
on silent watch, where Mr. Duckworth sat.

Spa Man

On her it looks ok, belt tied loosely
in a bow with a hint of cleavage,
soft cotton pile following her curves.
She should by rights be eating lettuce.

On me, I'm not so sure.
This masculine knot, the bathrobe tight
around my coarse skin and blackheads
my mother would home in on.
These protruding beefsteak calves.

In my imagination I could be a legionary,
the robe a segum keeping out the cold.
I could see myself as senatorial,
saluting, toga draped over my shoulders.

But, notice how I follow her, the frown
I do not always know I'm wearing,
the way my head is down, studying
my feet in these fluffy white mules.

First Time

She lived in the corner house,
where smooth macadam met the coral
of cobbled streets, doors all painted
in tropical reds and greens.

To enter her garden through the tall gate
with the latch that clicked
was to step into a high-walled sea,
long grass waving in the eddies of wind.

Once, in a dress as pink as a shell
she swam towards me, pressed dry lips
to mine, her round eyes staring, close.

Shocked, I flicked away, minnow-sharp;
fled through the shoals of leaves,
surfaced and beached in a new world.

TRIPTYCH

Nothing to shout about

Soon, I shall be a grandfather.
Inside I am still jiving,
and riding a Lambretta,
and you are on my shoulders
on the climb up Snowdon.

Granddad! I shall refuse
to wear the label,
to feel like a refugee
with a battered suitcase, remembering
the old country, the better times.

I shall not wear it
like a badge of pride,
boasting to neighbours,
to friends, to anyone who'll listen,
as if I had performed some kind of miracle.

No. You are the miracle,
the way you place my hand
on your distended belly
to let me feel an elbow,
his tiny thunderous kicks.

Through your tense abdomen
his little hiccups
are the sound of all Creation.
This touching is like being
in the presence of God.

And soon I am to be a grandfather.
Inside, this complete person
is lying ready, rolling over
to make himself more comfortable,
waiting his time.

Sentimental abstract e-mail poem

Hi Penny.

Sorry
but I won't be at the gathering tomorrow.
I'm in Edinburgh
with my first-born, just-born grandson
Hamish William.
He is wondrous. I look at him and stare
and stare again,
trying to make the wonderment
permanent.
Some days, abstract nouns are
where we live.

My daughter, who in the first flush
of motherhood
is torn and pale, seems young again
and vulnerable.
Today the oldest abstract noun of all
is everything.

See you at the meeting in February.

Bert

Something tight inside

My voice has a mind of its own.
In song it's as flat as a damp chapatti.
Notes lurch from flat to sharp.
Piano or strings seem too daunting,
and trapped in a sing-a-long I mouth or mime.

Yesterday I had a grandson – my first.
He is a kind of perfection – his cry
for food, mouth open wide, is elemental,
and today something tight inside relaxed
like an unsuspected catch springing open.

On impulse I bought myself a ukulele,
joined a uke group just for fun.
I'm told it's easy to play – only four strings,
a few chords to learn, and you can strum
a backing with one finger.

Suddenly I am making my own music,
bouncing out the rhythm of new life,
belting out the 'glory of the lord',
learning to rock-a-my-soul,
like a new-born discovering his lungs.